Thoughts, Moods and Ideals

Crimes of Leisure

W. D. Lighthall

Alpha Editions

This edition published in 2023

ISBN : 9789357941051

Design and Setting By
Alpha Editions
www.alphaedis.com
Email - info@alphaedis.com

THE CONFUSED DAWN.

YOUNG MAN
  What are the Vision and the Cry
That haunt the new Canadian soul?
  Dim grandeur spreads we know not why
O'er mountain, forest, tree and knoll,
  And murmurs indistinctly fly.—
  Some magic moment sure is nigh.
O Seer, the curtain roll!

SEER
The Vision, mortal, it is this—
  Dead mountain, forest, knoll and tree
Awaken all endued with bliss,
  A native land—O think!—to be—
Thy native land—and ne'er amiss,
Its smile shall like a lover's kiss
  From henceforth seem to thee.

The Cry thou couldst not understand,
  Which runs through that new realm of light,
From Breton's to Vancouver's strand
  O'er many a lovely landscape bright,
It is their waking utterance grand,
The great refrain "A NATIVE LAND!"—
  Thine be the ear, the sight.

(1882.)

NATIONAL HYMN.

To Thee whose smile is might and fame,
  A nation lifts united praise
And asks but that Thy purpose frame
  A *useful* glory for its days.

We pray no sunset lull of rest,
  No pomp and bannered pride of war;
We hold stern labor manliest,
  The just side real conqueror.

For strength we thank Thee: keep us strong,
  And grant us pride of skilful toil;
For homes we thank Thee: may we long
  Have each some Eden rood of soil.

O, keep our mothers kind and dear,
  And make the fathers stern and wise;
The maiden soul preserve sincere,
  And rise before the young man's eyes.

Crush out the jest of idle minds,
  That know not, jesting, when to hush;
Keep on our lips the word that binds,
  And teach our children when to blush.

Forever constant to the good
  Still arm our faith, thou Guard Sublime,
To scorn, like all who have understood,
  The atheist dangers of the time.

Thou hearest!—Lo, we feel our love
  Of loyal thoughts and actions free
Toward all divine achievement move,
  Ennobled, blest, ensured, by Thee.

CANADA NOT LAST.

AT VENICE
Lo! Venice, gay with color, lights and song,
  Calls from St. Mark's with ancient voice and strange:
I am the Witch of Cities! glide along
  My silver streets that never wear by change
Of years: forget the years, and pain, and wrong,
And every sorrow reigning men among.
  Know I can soothe thee, please and marry thee
To my illusions. Old and siren-strong,
  I smile immortal, while the mortals flee
  Who whiten on to death in wooing me.

AT FLORENCE
Say, what more fair, by Arno's bridgéd gleam,[A]
  Than Florence, viewed from San Miniato's slope
At eventide, when west along the stream,
  The last of day reflects a silver hope!—
Lo, all else softened in the twilight beam:—
The city's mass blent in one hazy cream,
  The brown Dome midst it, and the Lily tower,
And stern Old Tower more near, and hills that seem
  Afar, like clouds to fade, and hills of power,
  On this side, greenly dark with cypress, vine and bower.

AT ROME
End of desire to stray I feel would come
  Though Italy were all fair skies to me,
Though France's fields went mad with flowery foam
  And Blanc put on a special majesty.
Not all could match the growing thought of home
Nor tempt to exile. Look I not on ROME—
  This ancient, modern, mediæval queen—
Yet still sigh westward over hill and dome,
  Imperial ruin and villa's princely scene
  Lovely with pictured saints and marble gods serene.

REFLECTION
Rome, Florence, Venice—noble, fair and quaint,
  They reign in robes of magic round me here;
But fading, blotted, dim, a picture faint,
  With spell more silent, only pleads a tear.
Plead not! Thou hast my heart, O picture dim!

- 3 -

I see the fields, I see the autumn hand
Of God upon the maples! Answer Him
  With weird, translucent glories, ye that stand
Like spirits in scarlet and in amethyst!
I see the sun break over you; the mist
  On hills that lift from iron bases grand
    Their heads superb!—the dream, it is my native land.

[Footnote A: "Sovra'l bel fiume d'Arno la gran villa."—*Dante.*]

O DONNA DI VIRTU!

(DANTE—INFERNO, CANTO I.)

"O mystic Lady; Thou in whom alone
Our human race surpasses all that stand
In Paradise the nearest round the throne!
So eagerly I wait for thy command
That to obey were slow though ready done."

How oft I read. How agonized the turning,
  In those my earlier days of loss and pain,—
Of eyes to space and night as though by yearning—
  Some wall might yield and I behold again
A certain angel, fled beyond discerning;
  In vain I chafed and sought—alas, in vain,
From spurring though my heart's dark world returned
  To Dante's page, those wearied thoughts of mine;
Again I read, again my longing burned.—
  A voice melodious spake in every line,
But from sad pleasure sorrow fresh I learned:
  Strange was the music of the Florentine.

LINES ON HEINE.

I saw a crowded circus once:
  The fool was in the middle.
Loud laughed contemptuous Common-sense
  At every frisk and riddle.

I see another circus now—
  (The world a circus call I),—
But in the centre laughs the sane;
  Round sit the sons of folly.

IMITATED FROM THE JAPANESE.

"........................
I have forgotten to forget."—Japanese Song.
                    Tr. by R.H. Stoddard.

The morning flies, the evening dies;
  The heat of noon, the chills of night,
Are but the dull varieties
  Of Phoebus' and of Phoebe's flight—
Are but the dull varieties
  Of ruined night and ruined day;
They bring no pleasure to mine eyes,
  For I have sent my soul away.

I am the man who cannot love,
  Yet once my heart was bright as thine,
The suns that rove, the moons that move,
  No longer make its chambers shine;
No more they light the spirit face
  That lit my night and made my day;
No maiden feet with mine keep pace
  For I have sent my soul away.

O, lost! I think I see thee stand,
  By Mary's ivied chapel door,
Where once thou stood'st, and with thy hand
  Wring pious pain, as once before.
Impatient, crude philosopher,
  I scorned thy gentle wisdom's ray.
All vain thy moistened eyelids were;
  I sent my soul and thee away.

A causeless wrath, a mood of pride,
  Some tears of thine, and all was done;
On alien plains I travelled wide
  And thou wert soon a veiléd nun.
Not long a veiléd nun, but soon
  Unveiled of linen and of clay;
But I am March while thou art June,
  For I have sent my soul away.

And now when I would love thee well,
  There sits alone within my breast
Calm guilt that dare not from its hell

Look up and wish the thing thou art.
I see a dreadful gulf of fright
  Beneath my falling life; and gray,
Thy light becomes the ghost of light
  Above it as it falls away.

I have a life, a voice, a form,
  A skilful hand to lift and turn,
I have emotions like a storm,
  A brain to throb, a heart to burn;
But that which Jesus' blood can save,
  Which looks toward eternal day,
Is gone before me to the grave.—
  It was my soul I sent away.

The past is past, and o'er its woe
  It is no comfort to repine;
But I would wage my life to know
  Thy feet in heaven keep pace with mine.
I have no hope, I will not weep,
  The only wish that wish I may
Is this, that I may find asleep
  The soul I thought I sent away.

THE KNIGHT ERRANT.

CLOUD TO WIND
O blow, blow high, for I descend;
Friend must go to meet his friend,
If to earth you tie your feet
You and I will never meet.

WIND
Nay, I haste. A trifle wait;
I exceed my usual gait.
Ha! this hill-top is sublime,
But it makes me pant to climb.

CLOUD
Once again, a little space,
Meet we in this Alpine place,
Before you leap adown the vale
Or I along my pathway sail.

WIND
Then let our little bell of time
Ring onward with a chatty chime—
How we have fled o'er earth and sky,
And what you saw and what saw I.

CLOUD
O, I from off my couch serene,
Woods, meadows, towns and seas have seen;
And in one wood, beside a cave,
A hermit kneeling by a grave:—
The which I felt so touched to see
I wept a shower of sympathy.
And in one mead I saw, methought,
A brave, dark-armored knight, who fought
A shining-dragon in a mist,
That, mixed with flames did roll and twist
Out of the beast's red mouth—a breath
Of choking, blinding, sulphurous death,
On which I shot my thickest rain
And made the conflict fair again.
And from one town I heard the swell
Of a loud, melancholy bell,
That past me rose in flames of sound
And up to Saint Cecilia wound.

And on one sea I saw a ship
Bend out its full-fed sails and slip
So light, so gladly o'er the tide
I could not help but look inside—
Its passengers were groom and bride.
I floated o'er them snowily,
They felt my beauty in the sky,
Their eyes, their souls, their joy were one,
I would not cross their happy sun.
I love this life of calm and use—
No bonds but windy ribbons loose,
No gifts to ask but all to give,
Secure Elysium fugitive.

WIND
Your life, though, drinks not half the wine
Of active gladness that doth mine;
I spread my wings and stretch my arms
Over a dozen hedgéd farms;
I breast steep hills, through pine-groves rush,
Rock birds' nests, yet no fledgling crush,
Tossing the grain-fields everywhere,
The trees, the grass, the school-girl's hair,
Whirling away her laugh the while—
(We breezes love the children's smile);
And then I lag and wander down
Among the roofs and dust of town,
Bearing cool draughts from lake and moor
To fan the faces of the poor,
While sick babes, stifled half to death,
Grow rosy at my country breath.
I lent a shoulder to your ship;
I moaned with that sad hermit's lip;
I helped disperse the dragon's mist;
And some bell's voice, 'twas yours I wist,
I handed up to winds on high
Who wing a loftier flight than I.
But, hark! a rider leaves the vale.

CLOUD
Ah, yes, I catch the gleam of mail.

RANDOLPH
O speak again ye voicéd ghosts!
I heard afar your cheerful boasts.

And, if I doubt not, ye are they
That here have met me many a day.

WIND
We are they.

CLOUD, (echoing)
            We are they.
But whither now doth Randolph stray,
And why the mail, and why the steed?

RANDOLPH
This is my father's mail indeed,
Bequeathed with message to his son:
"Stand straight in it and yield to none."

WIND
But whither off and why away?

RANDOLPH
Off to the world; I cannot stay—
That world I have so often viewed
Here from this upper solitude—
This bulwark barring strife and trade.
Love calls me off. I love a maid,
Loving her silently and long,
Learning for her to hate the wrong,
   Learning for her to seek the right,
To hew at sloth and faint resolve
And thoughts that round but self revolve,
And pray for grace and virtue—wings
That bear men to the highest things,
   Enwrapt and rising into light.
For her, for her, O Cloud and Wind!
I trained my limbs and taught my mind,
Ran, wrestled, clomb, and learned to bend
The cross-bow with each village friend;
And by my hermit-guardian spent
The earliest dimness morning lent,
And the faint torch that evening bore,
In science and in saintly lore,
Reading the stars and signs of rain,
Noting each tree and herb and grain;
Each bird that flutters through the leaves,
Each beast, each fish that green lake cleaves,
The curious deeds Devotion paints

In missals and in lives of saints,
And every olden subtle trick
Of grammar, logic, rhetoric.
But most on chivalry I turned
A torrent eagerness, and burned
To hear of wrong repaired, or read
The working of some famous deed,
Like those I dreamt that I could do
When what I set myself was through:
Vexed lest the inward clock of fate
That ticked "Too soon!" might tick "Too late!"
But now that dial points the hour
When I must test my gathered power,
And leave my books and leave my dreams
Of steeds and towers and knightly themes,
Of tourney gay and woodland quest,
Of Perceval and Perceforest,
Of Richard, Arthur, Charlemain,
Amadis and the Cid of Spain—
Must leave them all and seek alone
Some grand adventure of my own.

CLOUD
Yet if you seek and cannot find
Or fail to work what you designed,
Be it but as the steadfast sun
Who bright or dim his course doth run,
And last doth reach as far a spot
Whether he seems to shine or not.

RANDOLPH
The height, the fynial of my aim
Is *to be worthy of her name.*

CLOUD
You mortals are a curious race—
More whirled by passions, hot in chase
Of passions, than myself am whirled
When tempests tug me o'er the world;
I cannot understand your ways.
We clouds live our divinest days
Beneath great sunny depths of sky,
High above all that you think high,
Drifting through sunset's surf of gold,
Dawn-lakes and moonlight's clear waves cold,

In realms so distant, chill and lone,
That Love, impatient, leaves the throne
To meditative Amity.

RANDOLPH
So would my guardian have it be,
So flowed his constant voice to me,
Of those to make me one, he sought,
Who watch from mountain towers of thought,
Or wandering into paths apart
Pursue the lonely star of art.

WIND
But you would rather love and do.
Well said, so much the wiser you!
But let your love be false as maid's,
Your every fire a flame that fades—
A word, a smile, an easy thing
To fledge and easy taking wing.
Kiss every lip, as tired of rest
As I am now. I'm off to west
Good-bye, and some day when you're hot
I'll meet you cool.

CLOUD
And I should not
Delay my showers so long as this.
God speed! Good-bye!

RANDOLPH
   Good-bye.
    I miss
Their wonderful companionship.
So onward seems the world to slip.
Now one glance backward firmly cast;
Thy next foot forward bears thee past
The mountain's crest. Ah, I behold
Our reckless river leaping bold
Down all its ledges. And I see
The castle where Elaine must be.
Lo, in yon window sits she oft.—
From yon green maze of willows soft
I hear our hermitage's bell.
Sweet sound, sweet many scenes, farewell.
  Elaine! Elaine!

CUJUS ANIMÆ PROPICIETUR DEUS.

A quiet, old cathedral folds apart
  At Oxford, from the world of colleges
A world of tombs, and shades them in its heart;
  Contrasting with the busy knowledges
This wisdom, that they all shall end in peace.—
"Vex you not, slaves of truth! there is release."

There every window is a monument
  Emblazoned: every slab along the pave,
Each effigy with knees devoutly bent,—
  Or prone, with folded gauntlets,—is a grave.
Unnoticed down the sands of Kronos run:
Slow move the sombre shadows with the sun.

Hard by a Norman shaft, along the floor
  A portraiture on ancient bronze designed
In Academic hood and robes of yore,
  Commemorates some by-gone lord of mind.
Mournful the face and dignified the head:
A man who pondered much upon the dead.

Repose unbroken now his dust surrounds,
  He is with those whom mortals honor most.
Respect and tender sighs and holy sounds
  Of choirs, and the presence of the Holy Ghost
And fellow spirits and shadowy mem'ries dear
Make for his rest a sacred atmosphere.

Sometime a gentle and profound Divine,
  Father revered of spiritual sons.
He died. They laid him here. About his shrine,
  Of what they wrote this remnant legend runs:
"Nascitur omnis homo peccato mortuus
Una post cineres virtus vivere sola facit."[A]

There as I breathed the lesson of the dead:
Sudden the rich bells chorussed overhead:
  "O be not of the throng ephemeral
    To whom to-day is fame, to-morrow fate,
  Proud of some robe no statelier than a pall,
  Mad for some wreath of cypress funeral—
    A phantom generation fatuate.

Stand thou aside and stretch a hand to save,
Virtue alone revives beyond the grave."

[Footnote A: "Every man is born dead in sin. Virtue alone brings life
eternal."]

STANCHEZZA.

EARLY LINES

Lo Zephyr floats, on pinions delicate,
Past the dark belfry, where a deep-toned bell
Sways back and forth, Grief tolling out the knell
    For thee, my friend, so young and yet so great.
    Dead—thou art dead. The destiny of men
Is ever thus, like waves upon the main
To rise, grow great, fall with a crash and wane,
    While still another grows to wane again,
    Dead—thou art dead. Would that I too were gone
And that the grass which rustles on thy grave
Might also over mine forever wave
    Made living by the death it grew upon.
I ask not Orpheus-like, that Pluto give
Thy soul to earth. I would not have thee live.

PRÆTERITA EX INSTANTIBUS.

How strange it is that, in the after age,—
  When Time's clepsydra will be nearer dry—
  That all the accustomed things we now pass by
Unmarked, because familiar, shall engage
The antique reverence of men to be;
  And that quaint interest which prompts the sage
  The silent fathoms of the past to gauge
Shall keep alive our own past memory,
Making all great of ours—the garb we wear—
  Our voiceless cities, reft of roof and spire—
  The very skull whence now the eye of fire
Glances bright sign of what the soul can dare.
So shall our annals make an envied lore,
And men will say, 'Thus did the men of yore.'

SUNRISE.

EARLY LINES

I saw the shining-limbed Apollo stand,
   Exultant, on the rim of Orient,
  And well and mightily his bow he bent,
And unseen-swift the arrow left his hand.
  Far on it sped, as did those elder ones
    That long ago shed plague upon the Greek—
    Far on—and pierced the side of Night, who weak
And out of breath with fright, fled to his sons,
  The nether ghosts; and lo! his jewelled robe
No more did shade a sleep-encircled world;
And thereupon the faëry legions furled
  The silk of silence, and the wheeling globe
Spun freer on its grand, accustomed way,
While all things living rose to hail the day.

REALITY.

A FANCY

Fade lesser dreams, that, built of tenderness,
Young trust and tinted hopes, have led me long.
These jagged ways ye whiled will pain me less
Than hath your falsity. Your spirit song
Sent magic wafted up and down along
The waves of wind to me. Your world was real.
There was no ruder world that I could feel.
I lived in dreams and thought you all I would,
Nor knew what dread, bare truth is doomed to rise,
When love and hope and all but one far Good,
Like sunset lands feel the cold night of lies.

Go, sweetest visions, die amid my tears,
For hence, nor cheered, nor blinded, must I seek
That larger dream that cannot fade; though years
Of leaden days and leagues of by-path bleak
Must intervene, with austere sadness gray,
Fade dimmer! lest in agony I turn,
And heartsick seek ye, though the Fates shriek "Nay!"
And the wroth heavens with judgment lightnings burn.

Go useless lesser dreams. And where they were,
Rise, grave aërial Good! Thy texture's true.
There is no good can die. "No ill," says Time, "can bear,
However beautiful, my long, long earnest view."

SEARCHINGS.

(EARLY LINES.)

Soul, thou hast lived before. Thy wing
  Hath swept the ancient folds of light
Which once wrapt stilly everything,
  Before the advent of a Night.

O thou art blind and thou art dead
  Unto the knowledge that was thine.
A longing and a dreamy dread
  Alone oft shadow the divine.

Full loud calls past eternity,
  But Lethe's murmur stills its roar,
The one vague truth that reaches thee
  Is this—that thou hast lived before.

Home often comes some voice of eld
  Confused and low—a broken surge
By fate and distance half withheld—
  Rich in linked sadness like a dirge.

The muffled, great bell Silence clangs
  His solemn call, and thou, O soul!
Dost stir in sense's torpid fangs,
  Like the blind magnet, toward a pole.

The deep, vast, swelling organ-sound;
  The cadence of an evening flute,
Bring oft those ancient joys around
  To linger till the notes are mute.

And when thy hushéd breathing fills
  The shrine of quiet reverence,
Then, too, a freeing angel stills
  The clanking of the chains of sense.

But nearest to that former life
  Another power calleth thee,
Away from care, away from strife,
  Toward what thou wast—infinity.

And in thee, soul, the deepest chord
  Thrills to a strain rung from above;
That strain is bound within a word,
  A sole, sweet word, and it is—Love.

Love—yet it cannot set thee free
  To sweep again those folds of light,
It torches but a part to thee
  And dim, though fair. The rest is night.

As the fine structure of a man
  Fits into life's great world, foremade,
So too it shadoweth the plan
  Of ages hidden in the shade.

And thou hast lived before; hast known
  The depth of every mystery,
Has dwelt in Nature, hid, alone
  And winged the blue ætherial sea;

Hast looked upon the ends of space;
  Hast visited each rolling star,—
Before Time measured forth his pace,
  Scythe-armed, on a terrestrial war.

HOMER.

(EARLY LINES.)

Time, with his constant touch, has half erased
The memory, but he cannot dim the fame
  Of one who best of all has paraphrased
The tale of waters with a tale of flame,
Yet left us but his accents and his name.

Upon that life, the sun of history
Shines not, but Legend, like a moon in mist,
  Sheds over it a weird uncertainty,
In which all figures wave and actions twist,
So that a man may read them as he list.

We know not if he trod some Theban street,
And sought compassion on his aged woe,
  We know not if on Chian sand his feet
Left footprints once; but only this we know,
How the high ways of fame those footprints show.

Along the border of the restless sea,
The lonely thinker must have loved to roam,
  We feel his soul wrapt in its majesty,
And he can speak in words that drip with foam,
As though himself a deep, and depths his home.

Hark! under all and through and over all,
Runs on the cadence of the changeful sea;
  Now pleasantly the graceful surges fall,
And now they mutter in an angry key
Ever, throughout their changes, grand and free.

How sternly sang he of Achilles' might,
How sweetly of the sweet Andromache,
  How low his lyre when Ajax prays for light;
(Well might he bend that lyre in sympathy
For also great, and also blind was he.)

We almost see the nod of sternbrowed Jove,
And feel Olympus shake; we almost hear
  The melodies that Greek youths interwove
In pæan to Apollo, and the clear,
Full voice of Nestor, sounding far and near.

A dignity of sadness filled his heart,
That sadness, born of immortality,
   Which they alone who live in art
Feel in its sweetness and its mystery,
Half-filled already with infinity.

Yea, Zeus was wise when he decreed him blind,
And wiser still when he decreed him poor;
   For insight grew as outer sight declined,
And want overrode the ills it could not cure,
Else rhapsody had lacked its lay most pure.

OUR UNDERLYING EXISTENCE.

O Fool, that wisdom dost despise,
  Thou knowest not, thou canst not guess
Another part of thee is wise
  And silent sees thy foolishness.

Yet, fool, how dare I pity thee
  Because my heart reveres the sages;
The fool lies also deep in me;
  We all are one beneath the ages.

TO _____.

"Creation—God's kind giving—
  Continues: did not at one Adam end.
New realms start open to each generation,
  Each man receives some gift, some revelation:
I, in this late age living,
  The gift, the new-creation of a friend.

TO A DEBUTANTE.

Thou who smilest in thy freshness,
  Bright as bud in morning dew;
Keep this thought in thy heart's bower
"Ever turn, like sunward flower,
  To the Good, the Fair, the True."

A PROBLEM.

Once, in the University of Life,
Remember and *Inquire*, my old Professors,
A question hard requested me to solve:
"How can man's love be great and be eternal
If Right forewarns he may be called to leave it:
Whether should Love rule Duty and be all,
Or Duty turn his back on sweet Love crying?"

I paused—then spoke, not having what to answer:
"Ye know, Professors, how to utter problems
And man perplex with his own elements.
Yet I believe the ways ye teach are perfect
And able are you what ye set to solve.—
Admiring you, however, aids me nothing,
I speak because I have not what to answer."
"Ponder," they said, those quiet, sage Professors,

I had seen Love—O Vision, I was near thee
When Death refused that I should speak with thee!
And I had seen her soft eyes' trustful brightness
Wondrous look down into the soul of many
And lead it out and make it of eternity.
Yes, truly, in her look men find true being!—
What ruin if such being must be withered!

I had seen Duty—soldier of his God—
Of Virtue and of Order sentinel—
Grand his firm countenance with obedience.
His troth to Love would everlasting be
Or nothing. What then should commanding orders
Bid him have done with her and all renounce?
How can he look on Love and know this shadow?

"I see no answer," answered I dejected,
"Except that either Love must be abased,
Or he resign perfection in his calling."

"Nay," said they, but by strange, clear apparatus
(Whereof within that College there is much)
Gave illustration—paraphrased as follows:
"Thou hast not reckoned for eternity.
The True fears not Forever: fear thou not.
Duty and Love are noble man and wife

(If otherwise thou see them 'tis illusion),
'Tis she sends Duty forth with dear embrace
And proudest of his battle through her tears
Encourages: 'Regard me not but strike!'
And 'If thou must depart alas, depart!
Follow thy noblest, I am ever true!'
He strikes and presses, sending back his heart
As forward moves his foot on the arena;
Or marches bravely far and far, until
Hope of return as mortal disappears:
This should true soul endure, though everlasting—
But then, besides, we know that One has mercy."

TO A FELLOW-STUDENT OF KANT.

The sweet star of the Bethlehem night
  Beauteous guides and true,
And still, to me and you
  With only local, legendary light.

For us who hither look with eyes afar
  From constellations of philosophy,
All light is from the Cradle; the true star,
  Serene o'er distance, in the Life we see.

TO THE SOUL.

AN ODE OF EVOLUTION

O lark aspire!
Aspire forever, in thy morning sky!—
Forever soul, beat bravely, gladly, higher,
And sing and sing that sadness is a lie.

Forever, soul, achieve!
Droop not an instant into sloth and rest.
Live in a changeless moment of the best
And lower heights to Heaven forgotten leave.

Man still will strive.
Delight of battle leaped within his sires.
They laughed at death; and Life was all alive:
In him not blood it seeks, but vast desires.

He wakens from a dream
Reviews the forms he fought in ages gone—
He or his ancestors, their shapes are one:—
And also of himself the forms he battled seem.

He sees the truth!
"I wrestled with myself, and rose to strength.
Still be that progress mine!—I see at length
All World, all Soul are one, all ages youth!"

THE PALMER.

O solemn clime to which my spirit looks,
No more will I the path to thee defer,—
Worn here with search—a too sad wanderer,—
The dance-tune spent, surpassed the sacred books,
And spurned that city's walls where I did plan
A thousand lives, unwitting I was pent;
As though my thousand lives could be content
With any vista in the bounds of man!

Eternal clime, our exile is from thee!
Flood o'er thy portals like the tender morn!—
Receive! receive! and let us new be born!
We are thy substance—spirit of thy degree—
Mist of thy bliss—fire, love, infinity!
And only by some mischance from thee torn.

THE ARTIST'S PRAYER.

I know thee not, O Spirit fair!
  O Life and flying Unity
Of Loveliness! Must man despair
  Forever in his chase of thee!

When snowy clouds flash silver-gilt,
  Then feel I that thou art on high!
When fire o'er all the west is spilt,
  Flames at its heart thy majesty.

Thy beauty basks on distant hills;
  It smiles in eve's wine-colored sea;
It shakes its light on leaves and rills;
  In calm ideals it mocks at me;

Thy glances strike from many a lake
  That lines through woodland scapes a sheen;
Yet to thine eyes I never wake:—
  They glance, but they remain unseen.

I know thee not, O Spirit fair!
  Thou fillest heaven: the stars are thee:
Whatever fleets with beauty rare
  Fleets radiant from thy mystery.

Forever thou art near my grasp;
  Thy touches pass in twilight air;
Yet still—thy shapes elude my clasp:—
  I know thee not, thou Spirit fair!

O Ether, proud, and vast, and great,
  Above the legions of the stars!
To this thou art not adequate;—
  Nor rainbow's glorious scimitars.

I know thee not, thou Spirit sweet!
  I chained pursue, while thou art free.
Sole by the smile I sometimes meet
  I know thou, Vast One, knowest me.

In old religions hadst thou place:
  Long, long, O Vision, our pursuit!
Yea, monad, fish and childlike brute
  Through countless ages dreamt thy grace.

Grey nations felt thee o'er them tower;
  Some clothed thee in fantastic dress;
Some thought thee as the unknown Power,
  I, e'er the unknown Loveliness.

To all, thou wert as harps of joy;
  To bard and sage their fulgent sun:
To priests their mystic life's employ;
  But unto me the Lovely One.

Veils clothed thy might; veils draped thy charm;
  The might they tracked, but I the grace;
They learnt all forces were thine Arm,
  I that all beauty was thy Face.

Night spares us little. Wanderers we.
  Our rapt delights, our wisdoms rare
But shape our darknesses of thee,—
  We know thee not, thou Spirit fair!

Would that thine awful Peerlessness
  An hour could shine o'er heaven and earth
And I the maddening power possess
  To drink the cup,—O Godlike birth!

All life impels me to thy search:
  Without thee, yea, to live were null;
Still shall I make the dawn thy Church,
  And pray thee "God the Beautiful."

THE WIND-CHANT.

The Soul, the inner, immortal Ruler.—*Hindu Upanishad.*

"Witch-like, see it planets roll,
  Hear it from the cradle call—
Nature?—Nature is the soul;
  That alone is aught and all.
Grieved or broken though the song,
  The fount of music is elate,
For the Soul is ever strong,
  For the Soul is ever great."

"For the Soul is ever great!"—
  Songless sat I by a grove,
Pines, like funeral priests of state,
  Chanted solemn rites above.
Dark and glassy far below,
  The River in his proud vale slept,
Eve with olive-shafted bow
  Like a stealthy archer crept.

Why, O Masters, then I thought,
  Is the mantle yours, of song?
Why with hours like this do not
  Glorious strains to *all* belong?

Why *all* choosing, why *all* ban?
  Why are lords, and why are slaves
And the most of gentle man
  Clipt and harried to their graves?
Foiled and ruined, masses die
  That one fair and noble be.
Why are all not Masters? Why
  So unjust is Life's decree?

Why are poor and why are rich?
  Why are slaves and why are lords?
Unto this the splendid niche:
  Those caste damneth in their words.
Do not powers of evil reign?
  Do not flashes' storms make dread?
Should not He of Life again

Bring the just peace of the dead?

Oft the Pines, like priests of state,
  Have spoke the heavenly word to man;
So above me as I sate
  Æol voices chanting ran:
"For the Soul is ever great
  For the Soul is ever strong;
In the murmurer it can wait—
  In the shortest sight see long.

"Not a yearning but is proof
  Thou art yet its aim to own:
Thou the warp art and the woof,
  Not the woof or warp alone.
Couldst thou drop the lead within
  To the bottom of thyself,
All the World—and God—and Sin—
  And Force—and Ages—were that Elf.

"With thy breathing goes all breath,
  With thy striving goes all strife,
In thy being, deep as death,
  Lies the largeness of all life.
The world is but thy deepest wish,
  The phases thereof are thy dream;
They that hunt or plough or fish
  Are of thee the out-turned seam.

"Helpless, thou hast every power,
  In thee greatness perfect sleeps—
And thou comest to thy dower,
  And thy strength perennial keeps.
Stir the Aeol harp elate!
  Make a triumph of its song,
For the Soul is ever great,
  For the Soul is ever strong!"

Rushings cool as of a breeze
  Amened to their litany;
In their pure sky smiled the trees;
  And no more was mystery.
Clear I saw the Soul at work,
  All through fair Saint Francis vale,
Beauty-making; like a dirk

Peering bright amid the mail.

Vital the dark River wound,
  Glassy in his cool repose;
Many a bird-like country, sound
  As the Soul-voice upward rose.
Then as in a glass I knew
  I was vale and town and stream,
Shadowed grove and northern blue
  And the stars that 'gan to gleam.

This was I, and all was mine.
  Mine—yea, ours—the grace and might,
With the lordship of a line
  That laughs at any earthly knight.
Ah, what music then I heard!
  What conceptions then I saw!
Master-thoughts within me stirred,
  And there flashed the Master-law.
Next them did the greatest shapes
  Of Angelo crowd in a dream:—
Vain the grace that marble drapes;
  A village mason's these did seem.

But—the light from Angelo's eye
  That so deeply eager burns
With its fierce sincerity!—
  Ah, the ancient saw returns:
"Greater artist than his art;"
  Meaning: greater yet than he
Is the vast outfeeling Heart
  In him lying like the sea.

With a sudden eagle-stroke
  How this truth can lift one wide.
Then he sees the sublime joke
  Of humility and pride;
For the Soul is *ever* great,
  The one Soul within us all:
One the tone that shakes a state
  With the helpless cradle-call.

Yes, that wonder of the Soul
  Is the riddle of it all,
And the answer, and the whole,
  Bright with joy that rends the pall.

Brother-man, I pray you stand,
  Hear a minstrel; but the song
If you do not understand,
  Pass and do not do it wrong.

TO CYBEL DEAR.

LOVE-SONG.

Though others plight for pride or gain,
  And mix the cup of love;
Theirs be the duller troth, the stain;
  Ours the sweet stars approve.
My riches, love, they shall be thou;
  My pride, thy love for me:
No diamond fairer decks a brow
  Than thine sincerity.

Though ours be tenements, not towers,
  Theirs, lawns and halls of ease,
Beloved, 'tis heaven, not gold, is ours,
  And the realities.
No sordid wish doth make us one,
  But love, love, love.
O surely, surely, that is done
  Which the sweet stars approve.

THE STILL TRYST.

How love transcends our mortal sphere,
  And sees again the spirit-world,
Forgot so daily. Thou art here;—
  I know thee, sweet—though fair impearled
Thy face in a far atmosphere
    To others,—hearing in the sea
    My love a-crying up to thee.

Thou by the surf, I on the lake:—
  Yet in the *real* world we meet;
And O, for thy endearéd sake,
  Love, all I am is at thy feet.
With thy life let me breathing take,
    And through all nature do thou see
    My love a-crying up to thee.

And with thine eyes shall I pursue
  Yon shower-veils from the sunset flying,
Blown mid clouds white and lurid-blue
  That crowd the rainbow's arch, defying
Him who in red death shoots them through.
    Look with me; in this pageant see
    My love all glowing up to thee.

See what I see, hear what I hear,
  I too am with thee by the wave—
One all the day, the hour, the year:
  Our trust of love shall be so brave,
We shall deny that death is here
  Or any power in the grave.
    I know thee; thou canst love like this;
    Be ours the endless spirit-kiss.

Dusk falls. How purely shines that star,
  Concealed while day was in the sky;
Life, love and thou not mortal are,
  Though atheist noon your world deny.
Dusk falls:—though in the west a bar
    Of bloom on evening's pure cheek be;
    In beauty thy love cries to me.

THE CHICKIEBIDS.

The chickiebids are in their nest
  Overhead,—
Dimpled shapes of rosy rest
  Curled a-bed.
Night has sung her spell, and thrown
  Her dark net round
Their heads; their pearly ears have grown
  Deaf to all other sound.

O of me how you are part,
  Babies mine!
Your hearts are children of my heart.
  The inner sign
Of my eyes lurks in your eyes,
  And your soul,
That so brims with Paradise,
  Stirs what wonders roll
Unsuspected in myself,
  Who had thought
Life half death, till childhood's elf—
  Sign of angels men shall be—
  Came and taught
A youth eterne within futurity.

THE CAUGHNAWAGA BEADWORK SELLER.

Kanawâki—"By the Rapid,"—
  Low the sunset midst thee lies;
And from the wild Reservation
  Evening's breeze begins to rise.
Faint the Kônoronkwa chorus
  Drifts across the current strong;
Spirit-like the parish steeple
  Stands thy ancient walls among.

Kanawâki—"By the Rapid,"—
  How the sun amidst thee burns!
Village of the Praying Nation,
  Thy dark child to thee returns.
All day through the pale-face city,
  Silent, selling beaded wares,
I have wandered with my basket,
  Lone, excepting for their stares!

They are white men; we are Indians;
  What a gulf their stares proclaim!
They are mounting; we are dying;
  All our heritage they claim.
We are dying, dwindling, dying,
  Strait and smaller grows our bound;
They are mounting up to heaven
  And are pressing all around.

Thou art ours,—little remnant,
  Ours through countless thousand years—
Part of the old Indian world,
  Thy breath from far the Indian cheers.
Back to thee, O Kanawâki!
  Let the rapids dash between
Indian homes and white men's manners—
  Kanawâki and Lachine!

O my dear!—O Knife-and-Arrows!
  Thou art bronzed, thy limbs are lithe;
How I laugh as through the crosse-game,
  Slipst thou like red elder withe.
Thou art none of these pale-faces!
  When with thee I'll happy feel,

For thou art the Mohawk warrior
From thy scalp-lock to thy heel.

Sweet the Kônoronkwa chorus
Floats across the current strong;
Clear behold the parish steeple
Rise the ancient walls among.
Speed us deftly, noiseless paddle:
In my shawl my bosom burns!
Kanawâki—"By the Rapid,"—
Thine own child to thee returns.

MONTREAL.

Reign on, majestic Ville Marie!
  Spread wide thine ample robes of state;
  The heralds cry that thou art great,
And proud are thy young sons of thee.
Mistress of half a continent,
  Thou risest from thy girlhood's rest;
  We see thee conscious heave thy breast
And feel thy rank and thy descent.

Sprung of the saint and chevalier!
  And with the Scarlet Tunic wed!
  Mount Royal's crown upon thy head,
And—past thy footstool—broad and clear
  St. Lawrence sweeping to the sea;
  Reign on, majestic Ville Marie!

ALL HAIL TO A NIGHT.

All hail to a night when the stars stand bright
  Like gold dust in the sky;
With a crisp track long, and an old time song,
  And the old time company.

Cho.—All hail to a night when the Northern Light
      A welcome to us waves,
    Then the snowshoer goes o'er the ice and the snows,
      And the frosty tempest braves.

The snowshoer's tent is the firmament;
  His breath the rush of the breeze.
Earth's loveliest sprite, the frost queen at night,
  Lures him silvery through the trees.

Yes, the snowshoer's queen is winter serene,
  We meet her in the glade.
Dark-blue-eyed, a fair, pale bride,
  In her jewelled veil arrayed.

Let us up then and toast to the uttermost
  Fair winter! we knights of the shoe,
And in circle again join hearts with the men
  That of old time toasted her too.

THE PIONEERS.

All you who on your acres broad,
  Know nature in its charms,
With pictured dale and fruitful sod,
  And herds on verdant farms,
Remember those who fought the trees
  And early hardships braved,
And so for us of all degrees
  All from the forest saved.

And you who stroll in leisured ease
  Along your city squares,
Thank those who there have fought the trees,
  And howling wolves and bears.
They met the proud woods in the face,
  Those gloomy shades and stern;
Withstood and conquered, and your race
  Supplants the pine and fern.

Where'er we look, their work is there;
  Now land and men are free:
On every side the view grows fair,
  And perfect yet shall be.
The credit's theirs, who all day fought
  The stubborn giant hosts:
We have but built on what they wrought;
  Theirs were the honor-posts.

Though plain their lives and rude their dress,
  No common men were they;
Some came for scorn of slavishness
  That ruled lands far away;
And some came here for conscience' sake,
  For Empire and the King;
And some for Love a home to make,
  Their dear ones here to bring.

First staunch men left, for Britain's name,
  The South's prosperity;
And Highland clans from Scotland came—
  Their sires had aye been free;
And England oft her legions gave
  To found a race of pluck,

And ever came the poor and brave
  And took the axe and struck.

Each hewed, and saw a dream-like home!—
  Hewed on—a settlement!
Struck hard—through mists the spire and dome
  The distant rim indent!
So honored be they midst your ease,
  And give them well their due,
Honor to those who fought the trees
  And made a land for you!

CANADIAN FAITH.

I.

In the name of many martyrs
Who have died to save their country,
Poured their fresh blood bravely for it,
And our soil thus consecrated;
In the name of Brock the peerless,
In the name of Spartan Dollard,
Wolfe and Montcalm—world's and ours—
The high spirit of Tecumseh;
Of the eight who fell at Cut Knife,
Bright in early bloom and courage,
When our youth leapt up for trial;
In the names of thousand others
Whom we proudly keep remembered
As our saviours from the Indian,
From the savage and the rebel,
Or from Hampton, or Montgomery
By Quebec's old faithful fortress;
And at Chrysler's Farm and Lundy;
And upon the lakes and ocean;
Or who lived us calmer service;—
Many is the roll, and sacred;—
In their names a voice is calling,
  Through this native land of ours!

Hark, for we have need to listen!
All our martyrs warn and shame us.
Do not let them see us cowards!
Why are all these faint-heart whispers
In the very hour of progress?

Tattles of disquiet vex us,
And among us are new enemies—
Cowards, weak, ignoble whiners,
Esaus, placemen, low-browed livers,
Traitors, salesmen of a nation.
Some would have us drop despondent
And convince us we are nothing.
(Us of whom ten thousand heroes
Hitherto to here have conquered
And we *must* be faithful to them!)

Some are hypocrites and cynics;
Some would wreck us; some would leave us;
Even in the hour of peril
Would the hand of many fail us;
They would almost make to falter
  Our old simple faith in God.

Therefore this appeal, O brothers,
Earnestly do I adjure you
  To believe and trust your country.

By the glorious star of England,
Shining mast-high o'er all oceans;
In the name of France the glorious;
In the world-proud name of Europe;
Whence you draw your great traditions;
  I adjure you trust your country!

By all noble thoughts of manhood;
By the toil of your forefathers;
By their sacrifices for you;
By the Loyalist tradition;
And your own heart's generous instincts;
  I adjure you be Canadian.

II.

"Is there a place, a work, a rank
  Our Canada is called to fill:—
She has but struggled till she sank
  Hers is it but to toil and till:
No seat among the peoples ours."—
So speaks the Tempter in our bowers.
So soft he presses on his bonds:—
But hark! a softer voice responds:

"Behold, Canadians, this your place,
Your task, your rank, in earth *and heaven*
To make you an especial race
  To God and human progress given."
Too holy is the task for jeers,
Too lofty to permit of fears.

Ignoble is the fear of loss;
  The call of honour *all* demands!
What thought those generous hearts of dross
  Who sowed our races in these lands?
Who blames the Loyalist of pelf?
Champlain, what cared he for himself?

Ignoble is the dread of harm:—
  Expurge it for a nobler creed!
Until we smile at all alarm
  Poor will be our Canadian breed.
He may not count on victories
Who will not die as patriot dies.

Ignoble the consent to take
  The light opinions of our worth
That strangers condescending make
  Who own not better brains nor birth:—
Children of men who toiled and fought,
Build your own fate; respect your lot.

Arise! Live out a larger dream—
  Your nation's that ye may be man's:
Advance; invent; improve; the gleam
  Of dawn for all illume your plans!
Greece lived! the world requires again
The lives of nations and of men!

THE KEERLESS PARD.

No, I'm a disappointed man,
  Though I've acted fer the best;
But I tell ye, stranger, what it is—
  The Occident's not the West.

Have I got the hang of the dialeck?
  Ye're nearer New York ner I
An' ye've seen th' latest litteracher
  This lingo's laid-down by.

What is Bret Harte now givin' us?
  How's the Colorado tongue?
Bret wuz the pard that run the West
  When I wuz East—and young;—

That is to say, three months ago.
  But now I must be grey,
Fer I've been out here so long I've lost
  The hang o' the Western way.

Way down thar in the State o' Maine,
  In mild Skowhegan town,
I pastured as a tenderfoot
  An' the clerk o' Storeclothes Brown.

Till I got to readin' *Roarin Camp*
  An' about that Truthful James,
Buffalo Bill an' Bloody Gulch,
  An' pistol-an'-poker games,

An' the pleasure o' shootin' justices
  An' sheriffs deeputies
An' the oncomplainin' public
  An' the gineral mob likewise.

Then I—wich my name is Dangerous Jake—
  (Leastwise when took that way)
Sloped unappreciative Brown
  An' follered the wake o' day.

An' here am I in Bismarck Jug!
  Fer an inoffensive spree—
Puttin' some buckshot inter the leg
  Of a pagan-tail Chinee.

Wot is the good of our churches
  Ef the Mongol's goin' ter rule?
An' how kin ye shoot the redskin
  When they're givin' him beef and school?

What are the Rockies comin' too?
  Well, *I've* acted fer the best.
But the only remark I've got to make, is—
  The Occident's not the West

THE BATTLE OF LAPRAIRIE. (1691.)

A BALLAD.

I.

That was a brave old epoch,
  Our age of chivalry,
When the Briton met the Frenchman
  At the fight of La Prairie;
And the manhood of New England,
  And the Netherlander true
And Mohawks sworn, gave battle
  To the Bourbon's lilied blue.

II.

That was a brave old governor
  Who gathered his array,
And stood to meet, he knew not what
  On that alarming day.
Eight hundred, amid rumors vast
  That filled the wild wood's gloom,
With all New England's flower of youth,
  Fierce for New France's doom.

III.

And the brave old half five hundred!
  Their's should in truth be fame;
Borne down the savage Richelieu,
  On what emprise they came!
Your hearts are great enough, O few:
  Only your numbers fail,
New France asks more for conquerors
  All glorious though your tale.

IV.

It was a brave old battle
  That surged around the fort,
When D'Hosta fell in charging,
  And 'twas deadly strife and short;
When in the very quarters
  They contested face and hand,
And many a goodly fellow
  Crimsoned yon La Prairie sand.

V.

And those were brave old orders
  The colonel gave to meet
That forest force with trees entrenched
  Opposing the retreat:
"DeCalliere's strength's behind us
  And in front your Richelieu;
We must go straightforth at them;
  There is nothing else to do."

VI.

And then the brave old story comes,
  Of Schuyler and Valrennes
When "Fight," the British colonel called,
  Encouraging his men,
"For the Protestant Religion
  And the honor of our King!"—
"Sir, I am here to answer you!"
  Valrennes cried, forthstepping.

VII.

Were those not brave old races?—
  Well, here they still abide;
And yours is one or other,
  And the second's at your side,
So when you hear your brother say,
  "Some loyal deed I'll do,"
Like old Valrennes, be ready with
  "I'm here to answer you!"

WINTER'S DAWN IN LOWER CANADA.

To each there lives some beauteous sight: mine is to me most fair,
I carry fadeless one clear dawn in keen December air,
O'er leagues of plain from night we fled upon a pulsing train;
For breath of morn, outside I stood. Then up a carmine stain
Flushed calm and rich the long, low east, deep reddening till the sun
Eyed from its molten fires and shot strange arrows, one by one
On certain fields, and on a wood of distant evergreen,
And fairy opal blues and pinks on all the snows between:
(Broad earth had never such a flower, as in my country grows,
When at the rising winter sun, the plain is all a rose.)
Then seemed all nymphs and gods awake—heaven brightened with their
smiles,
The land was theirs; like mirages, stood out Elysian isles.
Westward the forests smiled in strength and glory like the plain,
Their bare boughs rose, an arrowy flight, and by them sped the train.
But dream-crown of that porcelain sea, those plains of sunrise snow,
The green woods east, the grey woods west, and molten carmine glow—
A light flashed through the sappling wastes and alders nearer by,
Where Phoebus worked the spell of spells that ever charmed an eye,
His bright spears to the forest-flakes reached; that on their branches
lay,
And each shot back, as we sped by, a single peerless ray.
More bright than starry hosts appeared that vision in the wood
And flashed and flew like fire-flies in a nightly solitude,
A maze of silver stars, a dance of diamonds in the day:

Through many lives though fly my soul as on that pulsing train,
That sparkling dawn shall oftentimes enkindle it again.